Straight Talk About...
GANGS

James Bow

Crabtree Publishing Company
www.crabtreebooks.com

Straight
Talk About...

Developed and produced by: Netscribes Inc.

Author: James Bow

Publishing plan research and development:
 Sean Charlebois, Reagan Miller
 Crabtree Publishing Company

Project Controller: Sandeep Kumar G

Editorial director: Kathy Middleton

Editors: John Perritano, Molly Aloian

Proofreader: Adrianna Morganelli

Art director: Dibakar Acharjee

Designer: Shruti Aggarwal

Cover design: Margaret Amy Salter

**Production coordinator and
 prepress technician:** Margaret Amy Salter

Print coordinators: Katherine Berti,
 Margaret Amy Salter

Consultant: Susan Cooper, M.Ed.

Photographs:
Cover: © Catherine Yeulet/iStockphoto; Title Page: Petrova Maria/Shutterstock Inc.; p.4:gualtiero boffi/Shutterstock Inc.; p.6: Tatiana Morozova/ Shutterstock Inc.; p.8: Sam Cornwell/Shutterstock Inc.; p.9: ShutterstockInc.; p.10:Duncan Walker/ iStockPhoto.com; p.11: Andrzej Fryda/Shutterstock Inc.; p.12: David P. Smith/Shutterstock Inc.; p.16:Glynnis Jones/Shutterstock Inc.;p.17:Blazej Lyjak/Shutterstock Inc.;p.20:Yuri Arcurs/Shutterstock Inc.;p.22:Galina / Shutterstock Inc.; p.23:Ronald Sumners/Shutterstock Inc.;p.24: MANDY GODBEHEAR/ Shutterstock Inc.; p.25:imageZebra/Shutterstock Inc.; p.26: Andrey Bayda/Shutterstock Inc.; p.27: Samuel Borges Photography/Shutterstock Inc.; p.28: Pavel L Photo and Video/Shutterstock Inc.; p.30: Shutterstock; p.32: Edw/Shutterstock Inc.; p.33: Shutterstock Inc.; p.35: Monkey Business Images/Shutterstock Inc.; p.36: Gilles Dion/iStockPhoto.com; p.37: ksb/Shutterstock Inc.; p.38: Helle Bro Clemmensen/iStockPhoto.com; p.40: iofoto/Shutterstock Inc.; p.42:John Lumb/Shutterstock; p.43: Christopher Futcher/iStockPhoto.com

Library and Archives Canada Cataloguing in Publication

Bow, James, 1972-
  Gangs / James Bow.

(Straight talk about--)
Includes index.
Issued also in electronic format.
ISBN 978-0-7787-2185-7 (bound).--ISBN 978-0-7787-2192-5 (pbk.)

  1. Gangs--Juvenile literature. I. Title. II. Series: Straight talk about-- (St. Catharines, Ont.)

HV6437.B68 2013   j364.106'6   C2013-901019-X

Library of Congress Cataloging-in-Publication Data

Bow, James.
 Gangs / James Bow.
    pages cm. -- (Straight talk about...)
 Includes index.
 Audience: Grade 4 to 6.
 ISBN 978-0-7787-2185-7 (reinforced library binding) --
 ISBN 978-0-7787-2192-5 (pbk.) -- ISBN 978-1-4271-9068-0
 (electronic pdf) -- ISBN 978-1-4271-9122-9 (electronic html)
 1. Gangs--Juvenile literature. 2. Gangs--United States--Juvenile
 literature. I. Title.
 HV6437.B69 2013
 364.106'60973--dc23
                                      2013004907

Crabtree Publishing Company
www.crabtreebooks.com   1-800-387-7650

Printed in the USA/052013/JA20130412

Copyright © **2013 CRABTREE PUBLISHING COMPANY**. All rights reserved. No part of this publication may be reproduced, stored in a retrieval system or be transmitted in any form or by any means, electronic, mechanical, photocopying, recording, or otherwise, without the prior written permission of Crabtree Publishing Company. In Canada: We acknowledge the financial support of the Government of Canada through the Canada Book Fund for our publishing activities.

**Published in Canada
Crabtree Publishing**
616 Welland Ave.
St. Catharines, ON
L2M 5V6

**Published in the United States
Crabtree Publishing**
PMB 59051
350 Fifth Avenue, 59th Floor
New York, New York 10118

**Published in the United Kingdom
Crabtree Publishing**
Maritime House
Basin Road North, Hove
BN41 1WR

**Published in Australia
Crabtree Publishing**
3 Charles Street
Coburg North
VIC, 3058

CONTENTS

The metal door closes with a loud, final-sounding clang. Windowless concrete walls surround Brad as he sits on a cold metal chair in front of a metal table bolted to the floor. He is anxious. He finds it hard to breathe. He thinks about why he's here.

One package, that's all it was. Yet, here he is in jail, charged with selling drugs. The police know Brad was moving the dope for his gang. His friend, John, had asked Brad to deliver the package. Brad did as he was told. He didn't count on the police waiting for him.

One phone call. That's all Brad gets. But whom should he call? Brad hasn't talked to his parents in weeks. John made it clear that Brad should keep his mouth shut if the police arrested him. *You don't sell out your friends.* That's the code of the gang. Brad is in trouble. Where's John now? Good question. Some friend he turned out to be.

Introduction
The Wrong Crowd

People who join gangs are not all bad. Some, like Brad, just make bad decisions. Maybe they have problems at home. Maybe they feel alone and powerless. Maybe they just want to belong and have people respect them.

Gangs thrive in many cities, suburbs, and rural areas. Gang members appear confident and cocky. They flash wads of cash. They drive expensive cars. Those who join gangs may want to be rich and respected. They soon find out that the glamour of gang life is an illusion.

In a way, Brad is lucky. He's still young. He's arrested, but he's now less likely to die in a gang-related shooting. He still has a chance to straighten out his life. All Brad needs to do is get out of the gang. That's easier said than done.

"I've always been the kid that's picked on and made fun of. I started hanging out with this really tough group of girls. They're mean, and now people are afraid of me. They don't pick on me anymore."
Keira, aged 16.

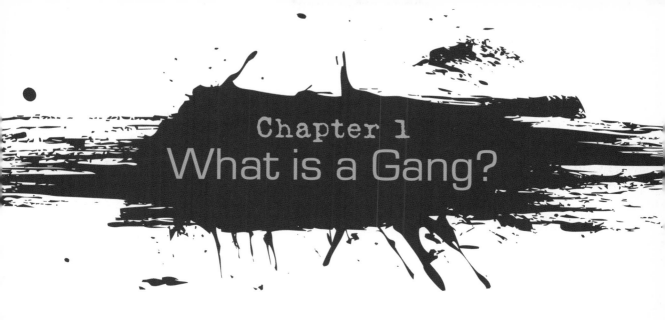

Chapter 1
What is a Gang?

We use the word gang to describe groups of people, or friends, who gather for a variety of purposes. A group of close friends is often called a gang. But that's not what this book is about. This book is about gangs that gather to do bad things.

This book is about dangerous and violent gangs. Such gangs steal and **vandalize** property. They sell drugs and commit murder. They threaten people and take their money. Such gangs are called street gangs, or outlaw gangs.

Gangs threaten not only communities, but often their own members. Young people who join gangs are ruining their lives. They are drawn away from their true friends. They stop going to school. They are targets for law enforcement. They can even be killed. For many gang members, the only way to leave the gang is in a body bag.

How do Gangs Form?

Many people join gangs because they see their future as bleak. They lack an education. They can't find good-paying jobs. A few join to feel safe in violent neighborhoods. Others join because they have few friends. Some join because they are bored. Others are pressured by their peers or family members. Some join gangs because they would rather do the victimizing than become victims themselves.

By the Numbers

Gang violence is a problem in every major city in the United States and Canada. According to the Federal Bureau of Investigation (FBI), gangs are responsible for 48 percent of the violent crime in the United States. While most of that crime occurs in the cities, the suburbs are not immune to the violence.

Source: Federal Bureau of Investigation

Gangs are responsible for much of the street crime in the United States and Canada.

Money-making Machines

Most street gangs are highly-sophisticated money-making machines. They sell and buy drugs. They commit robberies and thefts. They compel people to give them money. They force girls into **prostitution**.

That's why gangs are alluring for some people. In their view, the gang represents a perceived "good life." All this is an illusion. Gang life is hard.

In addition to living a life of violence, gang members, also known as gang bangers, find they have little independence. They are forced to take orders from the gang leaders. If they don't, they can face severe punishments, including beatings and death.

Drug trafficking is the lifeblood of most gangs.

By the Numbers

The FBI estimates that there are as many as 33,000 gangs in the U.S., with 1.4 million members. Most gang members are boys under the age of 18.

Source: Federal Bureau of Investigation

Gangs in History

Outlaw gangs are nothing new. They have been around as long as there have been people. In ancient Rome, for example, criminals banded together to rob unlucky travelers. Throughout history, society has **romanticized** outlaw gangs in fact and fiction, including the mythical tales of Robin Hood and his gang, and the real-life stories of desperados that terrorized the American West.

Outlaws ran wild in the American Old West.

Whether fictional or not, gangs operate outside the law, preying mostly on the innocent. Over the centuries, some gangs grew into powerful criminal ventures, including organized European crime gangs, the outlaw motorcycle gangs of North America, and the Asian **tongs**.

Powerful Criminals

Many gangs, such as the Irish Mafia or the Hell's Angels motorcycle club, grew so powerful that law enforcement had to expend vast resources to curb the criminal behavior. Some gangs grew so powerful that they controlled many aspects of life, including labor unions, manufacturing, construction, and trash-hauling.

Politicians have passed laws to reign in the power of criminal gangs. The most powerful came in 1970, when the U.S. Congress passed the Racketeer Influenced and Corrupt Organizations (RICO) Act. The law was written to stop the ill-effects of organized crime on the nation's economy. Police still use this mighty law to bring down many criminal gangs.

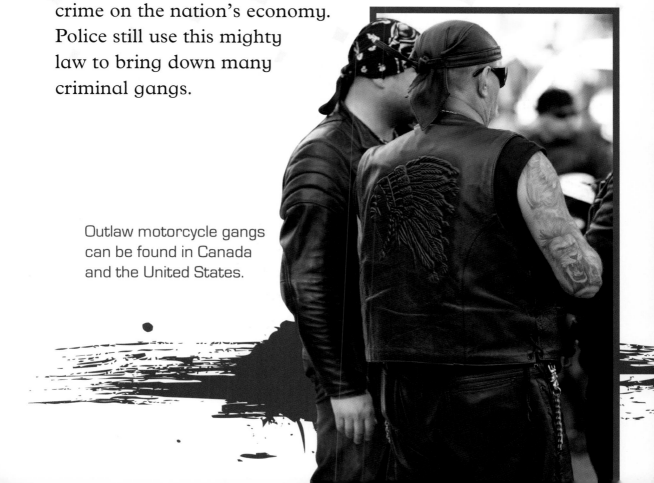

Outlaw motorcycle gangs can be found in Canada and the United States.

"I've always been called a 'troublemaker.' My parents even tell me I'm no good. When I first started hanging out with a gang, it was the first time I felt like I belonged, like I mattered." Jorge, aged 18.

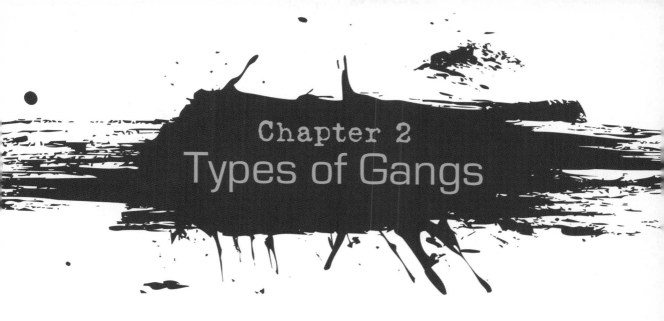

Chapter 2
Types of Gangs

There are three major types of criminal gangs. The first revolves around **nationality** or **ethnic** heritage. Perhaps one of the most famous areas for ethnic gang-related activity was in 19th century New York City. With its vast community of **immigrants**, New York became the hub of gang activity in the United States.

Much of that activity centered on the Five Points section of Manhattan. In this neighborhood, the Irish, Italians, Polish, and Germans had their own gangs. Sometimes they banded together to fight other gangs, or to control certain neighborhoods, such as the East River waterfront or the Bowery district.

Gang Definitions

The FBI has its own classification of gang types including:

- Street: Street, or neighborhood, gangs are formed on neighborhood streets.

- Prison: Prison gangs start inside the prison system. Members continue to commit crimes once they are released.

- Outlaw Motorcycle: Motorcycle gangs use their clubs as criminal enterprises.

- One Percenter: A One Percenter is a motorcyclist who uses the motorcycle club to commit acts of violence and crime. The group must include at least three people. There are 300 One Percenter Outlaw Motorcycle Gangs operating in the United States.

Prison Gangs

Prison gangs are another type of gang. When street gangsters go to jail, they don't stop being gang members. They continue their criminality in jail. Prison gangs run various illegal activities inside the prison walls. In addition, prison gang members often engage in crime and violence when they return to the community. Some gangs actually started in prison, and later moved to the street.

On My Turf

Turf gangs are another type of gang. Turf gangs generally live and control a specific territory within a community. A deadly war can often break out if rival gang members stray onto another gang's so-called "turf."

Bad to the Bone

Lawlessness is the trademark of every gang. In fact, the FBI says that in some areas in the United States, gangs are responsible for 90 percent of the crime. Gangs are involved in robbery. They deal drugs. They bring in guns. They're even involved in illegal gambling.

Most recently, gangs are branching out into non-traditional gang-related crime. Some gangs engage in **counterfeiting**. They illegally print money and sell cheap copies of popular clothing brands or electronics. Some gangs steal credit card and social security numbers.

Many gangs in the United States have links with Central American and Mexican gangs, forming a network to smuggle drugs across borders.

Moreover, gangs are now encouraging their members and their relatives to find legal employment in law enforcement to gather information on rival gangs and possible police actions.

Violence

Although making money is the chief function of a gang, violence is at the gang's core. Gangs use violence as a means of control. They use violence to commit crimes. They use violence to defend their territories. They use violence to **intimidate** other gang members, or the public.

"She was honest to God the funniest, prettiest and all around nicest person... I can't think of a single person who didn't like her and everyone loved laughing and joking with her. She had the nicest fun-loving attitude towards everything and I know that everyone will miss her."
a classmate remembering Jane Creba, an innocent victim of gang violence

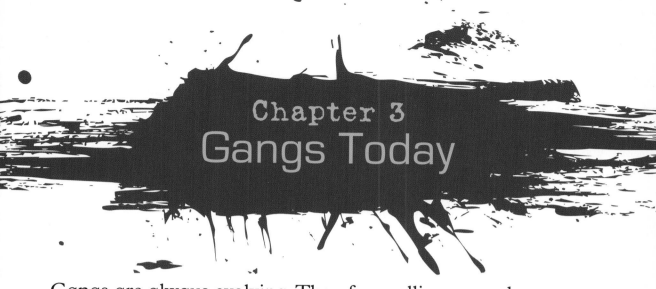

Chapter 3
Gangs Today

Gangs are always evolving. They form alliances and new associations. As each gang grows, so does gang-related crime. Girls and women are becoming more active in gangs. Sometimes, they form gangs of their own.

Gangs are also going high-tech. They use the Internet and wireless communication to hack into computers to commit bank **fraud**, identity theft, and credit card fraud. Gangs have begun recruiting technology-savvy members with the skills to commit these and other types of cyber-related crime.

Gangs are going high-tech, immersing themselves in the world of cyber-related crime.

Cybergangs

Gangs can use the online forums of Web sites to leave messages for gang members or other gangs. Texts sent out on cell phones are an easy way for gangs to plan quick meetings.

The police and other law enforcement authorities are finding the Internet useful in tracking gangs and preventing gang violence, however. They monitor Web sites. More than a few gang members have bragged about crimes on Facebook and Twitter, not realizing that the police were watching and reading.

In the Crossfire

Families, individuals, and entire neighborhoods are often in the crossfire of gang violence. Gangs make drugs readily available in neighborhoods. They bring guns to the streets. They make communities unsafe for people who aren't in gangs. Almost 25 percent of Canada's 611 murders in 2008 were the result of gang violence.

Gang members are much more likely to be killed or injured because of their activities.

Gang members live by a "code." The code tells a gangster what to do. For example, gang bangers are not allowed to talk to police. They also have to pledge obedience to the gang's leaders. Gangs demand loyalty, and punish those who don't give it.

Everyone's Problem

Some people believe that gangs are only inner-city problems, or occur in only poor neighborhoods, or are related to particular ethnic groups. Some people see gang violence as something that can't affect them if they live in the right area. These are all myths. Gangs operate in suburban neighborhoods. Members come from all cultures and ethnic groups. Innocent people are often affected by gang activity.

Consider what happened on December 26, 2005, in a popular part of downtown Toronto. On that day, two rival street gangs battled along a street crowded with holiday shoppers.

Gang members fired their guns. Four men and two women, none of whom had anything to do with the gangs, were wounded. A 15-year-old girl, Jane Creba, who was downtown shopping with her sister, was shot through the chest as she walked out of a pizza parlor. She died that day at the hospital.

By the Numbers

According to the U.S. Department of Justice's 2011 National Gang Threat Assessment, there are 1.4 million street, prison, and outlaw motorcycle gang members in the United States, representing 33,000 gangs.

Source: U.S. Department of Justice

"Moving into a new city I felt alone. I was jumped by this gang in school, and days later I stuck up for myself. The kids from another gang liked what I did and one thing led to another. I ended up becoming a member. Fighting made me feel like a man and I got mad respect for it." Malik, aged 18.

Chapter 4
Why Join?

Why do people join gangs? There are many reasons. Most join because they are unhappy with their lives. They come from poor neighborhoods where there are few good-paying jobs. A good education seems out of reach. The temptation to step outside the law and make more money is compelling.

Other people join gangs because they are bored. Even in rich neighborhoods, there aren't enough kid-friendly things to do. Parents are at work, not at home, and kids have a lot of time on their hands. Some teens turn to mischief as a form of entertainment. A neighborhood gang can provide an outlet.

Everyone has a desire to belong, even gang members. Many come from troubled homes where parents fight and alcohol and drug abuse is common. With no family to care for them, teenagers sometimes turn to gangs to give them a sense of belonging. They believe the gang is their family.

Only Way Out

People can feel despair when life is hard. They feel as if there is no way out. Every day, many teens are faced with extreme poverty. They live in neighborhoods where violence seems like the only way to solve problems. Kids see little chance of ever finding decent jobs or living in better neighborhoods. Kids join gangs because they think gangs are the way out of these miserable conditions.

Gang leaders feed off this despair. It gives them a group of people that they can **recruit**. Those who see no hope find it easy to do things that harm their community. In many ways, the despair that helps create gangs often fuels more despair.

Run-down neighborhoods are breeding grounds for gang activity. Crime, drugs, and guns are major problems in many of these areas.

We Want You!

People who join gangs enter a life of violence. Gang members are usually beat-in. Beat-ins are **initiation** ceremonies. During a beat-in, gangs welcome new male members by beating them up. Before girls are accepted as gang members, they are often forced to have sex with a number of gang members, or forced to fight a female gang member.

Beatings are a gang ritual.

Gang life is a risky business. Threat of arrest. Violence. Death. Guns. Drugs. All are all part of a gangster's life. The chance of arrest increases dramatically when a person joins a gang. Moreover, a gang member is likely to become a victim of violence.

Cliques and Gangs

What's the difference between a clique and a gang? A clique is a group, generally made up of adolescent girls. These girls exclude other people. Cliques may tease or bully to enhance their social status. Cliques are led by a specific person. The clique is an informal group, often seen as the "in-crowd."

Those in a clique can be bullies. They can taunt people they don't like. They can shun others. A clique is not a gang, however, unless the clique starts committing crimes. Most cliques don't do this.

Cliques can be socially devastating for those that are not allowed to join.

Gang Membership

According to the U.S. Department of Justice, gang membership is on the rise. This map represents the gang presence in each state based on population.

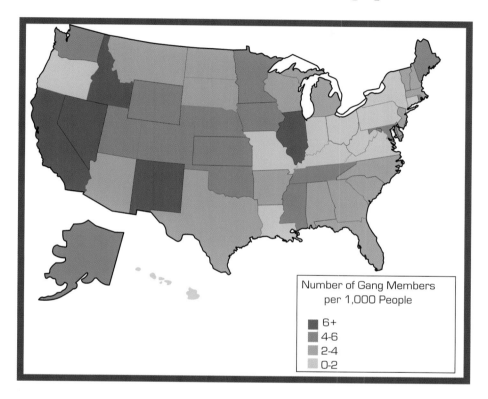

Number of Gang Members per 1,000 People

- 6+
- 4-6
- 2-4
- 0-2

Groups of Gangs

Outlaw gangs are everywhere. Nearly every community has them.

Juvenile gangs, for example, are a major problem in many areas, especially in Arizona, California, Connecticut, Florida, Georgia, Illinois, Maryland, Michigan, Missouri, North Carolina, New Hampshire, South Carolina, Texas, Virginia, and Washington.

In these states, juvenile gangs are responsible for the majority of crimes. They host parties, or organize special events, which allow them to recruit new members and to open up new opportunities for criminal activity.

Cultural and Ethnic Gangs

It's important not to **stereotype** gangs. They aren't limited to specific cultural or ethnic groups. In fact, many multi-cultural gangs exist.

However, a number of gangs do form along ethnic, racial, or cultural lines. A young person who moves with his or her family to a new country, for example, can sometimes struggle to find their place in a new unfamiliar culture. They may feel **isolated** and threatened, and associate only with other immigrants from their home country as a means of protection.

Ethnic gangs are spreading out from their home bases in major cities such as New York and San Francisco.

Every major city has had to deal with the problems caused by street gangs.

The Media's Role

The media often influences the formation of gangs. Newspapers, Internet news sites, and television provide coverage of gang-related crimes and activities.

When the media focuses its attention on the activities of gangs in a particular neighborhood or community, it creates the perception that these communities are unsafe. As a result, law-abiding citizens stay off the street, giving the gangs more territory.

Businesses won't open in certain areas, which pulls jobs out of the community. That in turn, increases the possibility that young people might turn to gangs for a source of income.

By the Numbers

Every city in the United States with a population of 250,000 or more has had difficulty with gangs, while 86 percent of cities with a population of 100,000 or more have had gang-related problems.

Source: U.S. Department of Justice

Hollywood Goes Violent

Hollywood plays a role, too. Some movies, music, television shows, and video games **glorify** gang-related activities. Studies suggest that before a child enters elementary school, they will have seen, on average, nearly 8,000 murders on television. By the time they turn 18, most teenagers have seen 200,000 acts of violence on television.

Some researchers blame gang violence, in part, on the media. They say gang members find it easy to be violent because they are constantly witnessing brutal images. Gang members, they say, become **desensitized** to the violence. As a result, they have no misgivings about committing acts of crime.

When you see something violent on television, it's worth asking whether the violence moves the story forward, or if the writers are using violence just to excite viewers.

Do violent video games lead to an increase in gang-related crime? Many experts believe so.

Myths About Gangs

Gangs are an inner-city problem, especially in African American and Latino neighborhoods.

Gangs are a problem in urban and suburban areas. Many ethnic groups, not just African Americans and Latinos, have their own gangs. Some are even multi-ethnic.

Only older teens are gang members.

Most gang members are male and range in age from 8-22. Gangs often use younger kids to run drugs or guns. If caught, these young gangsters generally do not serve long jail sentences.

Gangs are a way to get rich.

Gang leaders like to flaunt their riches. But the average gangster makes far less money than most people.

Gang violence happens only to those involved in gang-related activities.

Bullets, when fired, don't know the difference between a gang member and the innocent. Many of those killed by gang violence were innocents who were in the wrong place at the wrong time.

"I am now in prison ...arrested when I was 16. I ended any real possibility of having a successful life. When joining a gang, my outlook changed. I started to think I had no future because of the gang mentality." Tony, aged 25.

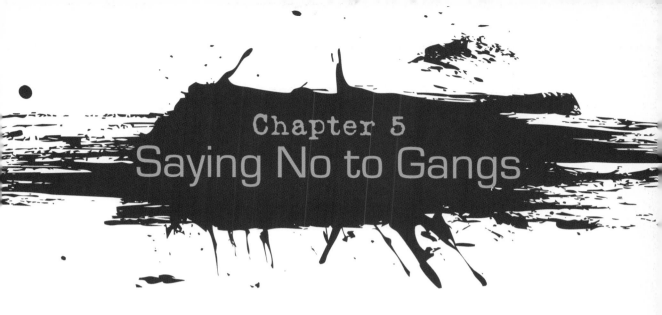

Chapter 5
Saying No to Gangs

Joining a gang will take away your sense of independence, threaten your safety, and the safety of your friends and family. It will also likely land you in jail.

People in gangs are at the top of the bad friends list. They're dangerous people. If you're thinking of becoming involved with a gang, ask yourself these questions: Do you feel safe around your gang friends? Will they really stick by you when things get rough? Are they taking advantage of you? What sort of activities are they involved in?

What will joining a gang add to your life? What do you hope to be doing in five years? What would your parents, friends, and teachers think about you joining a gang? If you don't like the answers to these questions, stay far, far away.

Friends in Need

Ask yourself the following questions if you think your friends might be getting involved in gangs. If you thought about joining a gang, they probably have thought about it, too.

- Are they changing friends? Are they becoming distant from you or other friends?
- Are they showing gang signs on their books, on their lockers, or on their clothes? Are they wearing colors associated with a gang? Are they wearing certain types of hats, or bandanas?
- Do they have tattoos? Are they using special hand signals to communicate with others?
- Is their behavior changing for the worse? Are they skipping school? Are they growing distant from their family? Are they using drugs or alcohol? Have you seen them carrying weapons or showing off a lot of money?

If you think a friend is involved with a gang, talk to him or her and try to help.

Testifying against members of a gang is courageous.

Pushing Back

Once upon a time, John Mendoza was one of the most notorious street-gang criminals in northern California.

In 2011, Mendoza decided to do something unheard of for a gang member—he ratted out his friends to police. As a police **informer**, Mendoza acted as a tour guide, taking **prosecutors** on a journey of Santa Clara County's underworld.

"What pushed me is I knew [the gang] had closed the door on me." Mendoza said.

How Do You Say No?

You might find yourself pressured into joining a gang or participating in a gang activity. You feel intimidated, not only because refusing excludes you from the group, but because you can become a target of the gang's wrath.

Saying no is always hard. But giving in is worse. The first step in avoiding gang activity is to refuse to do anything that is dangerous or makes you uncomfortable. Easier said than done, right? Here are a few techniques:

- *Say, "No, thanks!"* Often, it's that easy. Most people don't have a burning desire to force you to do something against your will. Saying "no" is often enough to end a situation.
- *Give a reason or excuse*. If the person keeps on asking, think of a reason not to do what they ask. You may have to make up an excuse. Whatever it is, say it confidently and without hesitation. Keep it short, and don't get into an argument.

By the Numbers

The president of the Chicago Crime Commission estimates that as much as two-thirds of school-related violence begins on social media sites. Arguments and online fights that start on such sites are carried out in the real world.

- **_Walk away_**. If the other person doesn't take no for an answer, walk away.
- **_Change the subject if you can't walk away_**. Talk about something other than what this person wants you to do. Repeat your excuses, for instance, or talk about something unrelated. When the time is right, walk away.

Gangs can be intimidating. You can do many things if you find yourself being pressured to join a gang.

Stay out of Trouble

These steps are useful if you find yourself in a situation where someone is asking you to do something you don't want to do.

- ***Try not to be there in the first place***. If you know where gang activity is taking place, don't go there. It will help keep you from becoming a target.
- ***Don't respond if approached***. Nothing says that you have to answer someone who asks you to make a bad choice. Turn away. Start a conversation with another person. Buy yourself some time so that you can find a way out.
- ***Stay close to friends you trust***. There is safety in numbers. Surround yourself with friends that make good choices. Be sure to stick up for them and support your friends' good choices, as well.
- ***Be assertive and confident***. If you show people that you won't be **manipulated**, they'll go away. Don't provoke a fight; clearly refuse, and get to a safe place as quickly as possible.

Standing your ground and being confident can help you in dicey situations.

Calling the Cops

Police are the first line of defense against a neighborhood gang.

Every day, in every major city and many small towns, police are on the frontlines trying to protect the community from outlaw gangs. If you see gang activity happening, you should first go to a safe place. Do not draw attention to yourself. You do not want to make yourself a target.

If you can, call 911. An emergency dispatcher will talk to you. They will ask you for some information that can help the police, firefighters, and ambulance crews. If you're a witness, talk to the police and tell them what you've seen.

If the situation is not life-threatening, or isn't obviously a crime, but you're still suspicious, call the police department's non-emergency line to report what you've seen.

The police will ask you for your contact information so they can follow up. If you know information about a crime, you can help police by calling Crime Stoppers. A special phone number allows people to leave tips anonymously.

"I told my gang 'sisters' that I missed out on a lot of school while I was locked up and I had to get my priorities together. I couldn't tell them that I just wanted out; they wouldn't accept that without putting their hands on me." Sue Lin, aged 17.

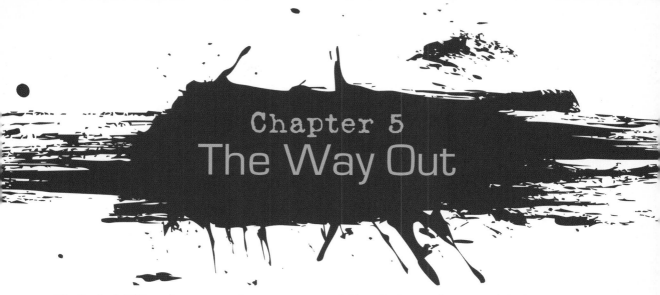

Chapter 5
The Way Out

Gabriel Hinojos got the tattoo while doing time at Folsom State Prison in California. It was a gang tattoo, a black teardrop, just below the eye. In the world of gangs, each inked teardrop stands for the time a gang banger spends in jail, or for a person he or she killed. Hinojos wanted the tattoo gone.

It was a painful process. Still, Hinojos wanted all traces of his gang life erased. The gang, Hinojos told a reporter, had been part of his life since he was 14.

A few years ago, Hinojos walked into an organization in downtown Los Angeles that provided job training, **GED** classes, and substance-abuse counseling. He found a job at the facility.

It took time, but Hinojos got his life straight, helped others overcome their problems, and even posed for pictures with the first lady. He vowed to stay out of the old neighborhood.

No Future

If you are a gang member, and if by some chance you're reading this book, then you have realized that there's no future in belonging to the gang. You know there's something better out there. Life does offer up second chances.

Leaving a gang is difficult, but it can be done. Death is not the only way out. Leaving can be a slow process. The lure of the gang is intense, but how do you leave—and stay gone? It can be complicated, but it can be done.

Certain tattoos are a tell-tale sign that a person has been in a gang. Most employers will not hire an individual if they have such tattoos.

Getting Support

Many factors make it difficult to leave a gang, as Gabriel Hinojos found out. Yet, many people safely leave gangs every day. How is it done? The list of steps below will help you leave and stay out of a gang.

- Never tell the gang that you plan to leave. You might pay with your life.
- Stop dressing like a gangster.
- Make excuses. Your fellow gang bangers will want to know why you haven't been around.
- Find support. Many people and organizations will help you leave.
- Go back to school. Many schools have special programs that help reduce the influence of gangs. Teachers and other school professionals don't want to see the children they teach fall under the influence of gangs. If you are in trouble with the police, they will **advocate** for you.
- Turn to family members. An older brother or sister, an aunt or uncle, or even a grandmother, can often help you escape the lifestyle. They can give you a safe place to stay, which makes it a lot easier to get off the street. A good home will make it easier for you to concentrate on going back to school, getting a job, and getting your life back in order.

- Ask a police officer or a social worker for help. The police, along with social workers in a number of cities and states, run programs that help keep kids out of gangs.
- Find resources in your community. Many towns and cities fund special projects giving kids a safe haven to hang out at after school. These programs also provide tutoring. Supervised spaces that teenagers enjoy using, such as basketball courts at community centers, have proven successful in keeping kids from joining gangs.

It's not easy to leave a gang, but it can be done. The key is to not go down that road alone. Find someone who can help.

Final Step

Victor Rios was a gang member arrested and beaten by police after stealing a car when he was 14. Today, he is an associate professor of sociology at the University of California, Santa Barbara. He describes his experiences in his book *Punished: Policing the Lives of Black and Latino Boys.*

Thanks to a teacher, a number of social workers, and a kind police officer, Rios was able to leave the gang, finish high school, and go to college. It wasn't easy. There were times when he almost slipped back into the lifestyle. Thanks to the help he received from the people who cared about him, he **persevered**.

"It dawned on us that by the time we reached our early twenties, none of the homies had avoided incarceration… out of sixty-eight homies, only two of us graduated from high school, and only I had made it to college…"

Gangs can make a person's life a nightmare, but with the right help, and a good education, a person can have a second chance.

Hot Topics
Q&A

There are many problems in my community. There's a lot of crime. There are no jobs. There's no way I can go to college. The gang is the only way out. What's wrong with that?

A: It is horrible to live in a place with so little opportunity. It's easy to see why the gang may offer the illusion of help. However, that's just what it is—an illusion. By joining a gang, your life expectancy goes down, as do your opportunities. You're more likely to go to prison.

I think my sister is getting involved with a gang. What should I do?

A: Consider the warning signs in this book. If you're still worried, talk to your sister about your concern. Even if she doesn't want your help, give it to her anyways. Talk to your parents, another family member, a teacher, or a school counselor. You might even have to talk to the police. Whatever you decide, make sure you let your sister know that you will always be there for her.

How can I help my community fight gangs?

A: Talk to your community leaders, and become a community leader yourself. In your community, there are people who are trying to make things better. They may be on a city council, or they might volunteer at a local community center or church. You'll find that there's a lot you can do.

Being in a gang sounds like fun. Is it?

A: At first, gang life seems like a good time. You're doing what you want, after all, and that is always fun. Remember, though, there's a price to pay. One gang member named Richard wrote about his experiences. He said gang life was fun. Then his little brother was killed and most of his "homeboys" were arrested. Then he got arrested. Membership in a gang might seem fun at first, but it's a lifetime of pain.

I'm going to have a baby and my boyfriend is in a gang. What should I do?

A: If your boyfriend doesn't want to get out of the gang, then he doesn't want to be responsible for the life of your baby. That responsibility will probably fall on you. The best thing to do is seek help, either with family members, a teacher, or some other trusted adult. Try your hardest to stay in school. You need to focus on yourself and your child. It will be hard to do that if your boyfriend doesn't leave the gang. You have to think of your child first.

Other Resources

There is plenty of information about gangs. You might find that a lot of the information repeats itself. You might also notice that some of it is not very reliable. Here are some sources you should find helpful. Web sites contain information that is useful in Canada and the United States. Telephone numbers and referral services are good in either Canada or the United States, but not both. If you do call a number outside of your area, the helpline will probably refer you to a number inside your region.

In the United States
The National Crime Prevention Council
1-202-466-6272
www.ncpc.org
Helps keep people, their families, and their communities safe from crime by providing tools to engage the community and help them find ways to make streets safer.

Covenant House
www.nineline.org
The group offers confidential advice for kids experiencing problems, including those that are gang-related.

In Canada

The Streets Don't Love You Back
www.thestreetsdontloveyouback.ning.com
A movement striving to educate youth about the dangers
of gang violence, drugs, and living on the street.

Gangs and At-Risk Kids
www.gangsandkids.com
Features stories by ex-gang members or gang members serving
long prison terms.

Gang Prevention
www.gangprevention.ca/youth
A Web site that not only offers information about gangs in British
Columbia, but also provides ways to prevent teenagers from getting
involved in gangs.

Hotlines

Arlington County, Virginia
(703) 228-GANG (4264)

Covenant House
1-800-999-9999

Youth Against Violence Line
1-800-680-4264

Crime Stoppers (Canada)
1-800-222-8477

Glossary

advocate Speak out in favor of something or someone

confident Sure of yourself

counterfeiting To copy something in order to defraud or deceive

desensitized To have experienced so much of something that one hardly notices it anymore

ethnic Being part of an identifiable racial group, such as European, African, Asian, Indian

fraud An act of deceiving

GED Short for General Equivalency Diploma

glorify To bestow honor

illusion Misleading image

immigrants A person who comes to another country and becomes a permanent resident

informer A person who gives information about an individual or crime to police

initiation A ceremony or a ritual before being accepted by a group or gang

intimidate Making someone feel threatened

isolated Alone

manipulated Controlled or influenced somebody in an ingenious or devious way

nationality Coming from another nation; a person from a family of people born in another country

persevered Persisted steadily in an action or belief, usually over a long period

prosecutors Attorneys representing the state or the people in a criminal trial

prostitution The act of engaging in sexual intercourse or other sex acts for money

recruit Enlist a new member into a group

romanticized Having no basis in fact

stereotype Oversimplified opinion of a group

tongs Asian, or Chinese, gangs

vandalize Deface, destroy, or otherwise damage, public or private property in a deliberate, malicious way

Index